ROYAL COURT

Royal Court Theatre presents

FLESH WOUND

by **Ché Walker**

First performance at the Royal Court Jerwood Theatre Upstairs
Sloane Square, London on 15 May 2003.

Supported by Jerwood New Playwrights

JERWOOD
NEW PLAYWRIGHTS

FLESH WOUND

by **Ché Walker**

Cast in order of appearance

Deirdra **Tamzin Outhwaite**
Joseph **Michael Attwell**
Vincent **Andrew Tiernan**

Director **Wilson Milam**
Designer **Dick Bird**
Lighting Designer **Neil Austin**
Sound Designer **Ian Dickinson**
Casting **Amy Ball**
Production Manager **Sue Bird**
Stage Managers **Kathryn Bools, Sarah Hunter**
Costume Supervisor **Iona Kenrick**
Company Voice Work **Patsy Rodenburg**

THE COMPANY

Ché Walker (writer)
For the Royal Court: Been So Long.

Michael Attwell
For the Royal Court: No One Sees the Video.
Other theatre includes: The Woman Who Cooked
Her Husband (New Ambassadors); The Man Who
Had All the Luck (Sheffield Crucible); The Colour of
Justice (Tricycle & tour); Arsenic and Old Lace
(Lyceum, Edinburgh); Sunday in Park with George
(RNT); Oliver (Albery); Richard III (Young Vic);
Satie Day/Night (Lyric Studio); The Strongest Man
in the World, Rabelais (Roundhouse); Androcles and
the Lion (Bristol Old Vic); Irma La Douce, City
Sugar, Sleuth, The Caretaker, The Norman
Conquests, Butley, Guys and Dolls (Leicester
Haymarket); Threepenny Opera, Rosencrantz and
Guildenstern (Newcastle Playhouse).
Television includes: The Great Industrial Wonders,
Daniel Deronda, My Family, Hope and Glory 11,
Border Cafe, Monsignor Renard, The Colour of
Justice, Casualty, Wycliffe, Silent Witness, Pie in the
Sky, The Bill, Poldark, Bugs, In the Dark, Anna Lee,
Spread Eagle, Harry 11, London's Burning, Scarlet
and Black, West Beach, Boon, Singles, Redemption,
The Paradise Club, Inspector Morse, Gentry,
EastEnders, The Chinese Detective, Bergerac,
Jemima Shore Investigates, Minder, Doctor Who,
King and Castle, Oliver Twist, Turtle's Progress.
Film includes: Circus, New Year's Day, Bodywork,
Hostile Waters, Tom and Viv, Horse Opera, Buster,
Masada, The Tenth Man, Joseph.

Neil Austin (lighting designer)
For the Royal Court: Trust.
Other theatre includes: A Prayer for Owen
Meany, The Walls (RNT); Further than the
Furthest Thing (RNT & international tour);
Caligula (Donmar); Japes (Theatre Royal,
Haymarket); Monkey! (Young Vic & tour);
American Buffalo (Royal Exchange,
Manchester); The Lady in the Van, Pretending
to be Me (West Yorkshire Playhouse); Romeo
& Juliet, Twelfth Night (Liverpool Playhouse);
Mr Placebo (Traverse, Edinburgh/Drum,
Plymouth); Great Expectations (Bristol Old
Vic); Loves Work, Cuckoos, Venecia,
Marathon, Une Tempête (Gate); Closer
(Teatro Broadway, Buenos Aires); Adugna
Dance Project (Street Symphony, Addis
Ababa).
Opera includes: The Embalmer (Almeida
Opera), Orfeo (Opera City, Tokyo & Japanese
tour), Pulse Shadows (Queen Elizabeth Hall),
L'enfant Prodigue, Le Portrait de Manon, La
Navarraise (Guildhall).
Musicals include: Babes in Arms (International
Festival of Musical Theatre, Cardiff), Spend
Spend Spend (tour, co-design with Mark
Henderson), My Fair Lady (Teatro Nacionale,
Buenos Aires), Rags (Guildhall), Cabaret
(MacOwan Theatre).

Dick Bird (designer)
Theatre includes: Great Expectations (Bristol
Old Vic); Peepshow, Heavenly (Frantic
Assembly tour); Ben-Hur (BAC); A Prayer for
Owen Meany, The Walls (RNT); The Lady in
the Van (West Yorkshire Playhouse); The
Lucky Ones (Hampstead); Misconceptions
(Derby Playhouse/Salisbury Playhouse);
Monkey!, The Three Musketeers (Young Vic)
Poseidon, Vagabondage, Half Machine,
Hunger I & III (Primitive Science); The
Invisible College (Salzberg Festival); Light
(Theatre de Complicite tour/Almeida);
Marathon, Une Tempête (Gate); Lucky You,
Snow Shoes (Royal Exchange, Manchester &
tour); Closer (Teatro Broadway, Buenos
Aires); My Fair Lady (Teatro Nacionale,
Buenos Aires).
Opera and dance includes: Messalina
(Battignano Opera Festival), Il Tabarro, Vollo
di Notte (Long Beach Opera); The Banquet
(Protein Dance, The Place & tour).

Ian Dickinson (sound designer)
For the Royal Court: Hitchcock Blonde, Black Milk, Crazyblackmuthafuckin'self, Caryl Churchill Season, Imprint, Mother Teresa is Dead, Push Up, Workers Writes, Fucking Games, Herons, Cutting Through the Carnival.
Other theatre includes: Port (Royal Exchange Manchester); Night of the Soul (RSC Barbican); Eyes of the Kappa (Gate); Crime and Punishment in Dalston (Arcola Theatre); Search and Destroy (New End, Hampstead); Phaedra, Three Sisters, The Shaughraun, Writer's Cramp (Royal Lyceum, Edinburgh); The Whore's Dream (RSC Fringe, Edinburgh); As You Like It, An Experienced Woman Gives Advice, Present Laughter, The Philadelphia Story, Wolks World, Poor Superman, Martin Yesterday, Fast Food, Coyote Ugly, Prizenight (Royal Exchange, Manchester).
Ian is Head of Sound at the Royal Court.

Wilson Milam (director)
Theatre includes: Mr Placebo (Traverse); Lieutenant of Inishmore (RSC Stratford upon Avon/The Pit/Garrick); On Such as We (Abbey, Dublin); A Lie of the Mind (Donmar); The Wexford Trilogy (Tricycle/Lowry/Gateway); Hurlyburly (Old Vic/Queen's); Bug (Gate/Woolly Mammoth Theater, Washington DC); Killer Joe(Vaudeville /Bush/Traverse/Soho Playhouse, New York/29th St Repertory Theater, New York/Lincoln Park Theater, Chicago/Next Theater, Chicago); Closer (Berkeley Repertory Theater, San Francisco); Pot Mom (Steppenwolf Theater Company, Chicago); The Caine Mutiny Court Martial (Red Orchid Theater, Chicago); Skeleton (Shattered Globe Theater, Chicago); Witness to Temptation American Blues Theater, Chicago).

Tamzin Outhwaite
Theatre includes: Baby on Board, Absent Friends, They're Playing Our Song (Stephen Joseph, Scarborough); Oliver (Palladium); Grease (Dominion); Carousel (RNT); Radio Times (Birmingham Rep & West End).
Television includes: Final Demand, Red Cap, EastEnders.
Film includes: Out of Control (won the Michael Powell Best Feature Edinburgh Festival 2002/RTS Award 2003/Broadcast Award 2003).

Andrew Tiernan
Theatre includes: A Lie of the Mind, The Bullet (Donmar); Noise (Soho); The Dispute (Crucible, Sheffield).
Television includes: Rehab, William & Mary, McCready and Daughter, A&E, Bulla, Hawkins, In a Land of Plenty, Four Fathers, Hornblower, Macbeth on the Estate, The Sculptress, Some Kind of Life, Cracker, Safe, 99-1, Middlemarch, Prime Suspect 11, The Guilty, Thacker, Prime Suspect.
Film includes: The Pianist, The Red Siren, Mr In-Between, The Bunker, The Criminal, Face, The Scarlet Tunic, Playing God, Lock Stock & Two Smoking Barrels, Small Time Obsession, Snow White in the Black Forest, Interview with the Vampire, Two Deaths, Being Human, The Trial, As You Like It, Edward 11.

ROYAL COURT
JERWOOD THEATRE DOWNSTAIRS

12 June - 12 July 2003
FALLOUT
by **Roy Williams**

A boy is found dead. D.C. Joe Stephens must return to his old neighbourhood to investigate. Shanice is avoiding his questions about her boyfriend Emile, and his mates. Ronnie saw something, but promised Shanice she'd say nothing. But when a reward is offered, keeping quiet becomes a major test of their street loyalty.

Directed by **Ian Rickson**
Design: **Ultz**
Sound: **Ian Dickinson**
Music: **Stephen Warbeck**

Cast **Lorraine Brunning, O-T Fagbenle, Lennie James, Petra Letang, Marcel McCalla, Michael Obiora, Daniel Ryan, Ony Uhiara, Clive Wedderburn.**

Supported by Jerwood New Playwrights

Box Office 020 7565 5000
www.royalcourttheatre.com

THE ENGLISH STAGE COMPANY AT THE ROYAL COURT

The English Stage Company at the Royal Court opened in 1956 as a subsidised theatre producing new British plays, international plays and some classical revivals.

The first artistic director George Devine aimed to create a writers' theatre, 'a place where the dramatist is acknowledged as the fundamental creative force in the theatre and where the play is more important than the actors, the director, the designer'. The urgent need was to find a contemporary style in which the play, the acting, direction and design are all combined. He believed that 'the battle will be a long one to continue to create the right conditions for writers to work in'.

Devine aimed to discover 'hard-hitting, uncompromising writers whose plays are stimulating, provocative and exciting'. The Royal Court production of John Osborne's Look Back in Anger in May 1956 is now seen as the decisive starting point of modern British drama and the policy created a new generation of British playwrights. The first wave included John Osborne, Arnold Wesker, John Arden, Ann Jellicoe, N F Simpson and Edward Bond. Early seasons included new international plays by Bertolt Brecht, Eugène Ionesco, Samuel Beckett, Jean-Paul Sartre and Marguerite Duras.

The theatre started with the 400-seat proscenium arch Theatre Downstairs, and then in 1969 opened a second theatre, the 60-seat studio Theatre Upstairs. Some productions transfer to the West End, such as Caryl Churchill's Far Away, Conor McPherson's The Weir, Kevin Elyot's Mouth to Mouth and My Night With Reg. The Royal Court also co-produces plays which have transferred to the West End or toured internationally, such as Sebastian Barry's The Steward of Christendom and Mark Ravenhill's Shopping and Fucking (with Out of Joint), Martin McDonagh's The Beauty Queen Of Leenane (with Druid Theatre Company), Ayub Khan-Din's East is East (with Tamasha Theatre Company, and now a feature film).

Since 1994 the Royal Court's artistic policy has again been vigorously directed to finding and producing a new generation of playwrights. The writers include Joe Penhall, Rebecca Prichard, Michael Wynne, Nick Grosso, Judy Upton, Meredith Oakes, Sarah Kane, Anthony Neilson, Judith Johnson, James Stock, Jez Butterworth, Marina Carr, Phyllis Nagy, Simon Block, Martin McDonagh, Mark Ravenhill, Ayub Khan-Din, Tamantha Hammerschlag, Jess Walters, Che Walker, Conor McPherson, Simon Stephens,

photo: Andy Chopping

Richard Bean, Roy Williams, Gary Mitchell, Mick Mahoney, Rebecca Gilman, Christopher Shinn, Kia Corthron, David Gieselmann, Marius von Mayenburg, David Eldridge, Leo Butler, Zinnie Harris, Grae Cleugh, Roland Schimmelpfennig, DeObia Oparei, Vassily Sigarev and The Presnyakov Brothers. This expanded programme of new plays has been made possible through the support of A.S.K Theater Projects, the Jerwood Charitable Foundation, the American Friends of the Royal Court Theatre and many in association with the Royal National Theatre Studio.

In recent years there have been record-breaking productions at the box office, with capacity houses for Caryl Churchill's A Number, Jez Butterworth's The Night Heron, Rebecca Gilman's Boy Gets Girl, Kevin Elyot's Mouth To Mouth, David Hare's My Zinc Bed and Conor McPherson's The Weir, which transferred to the West End in October 1998 and ran for nearly two years at the Duke of York's Theatre.

The newly refurbished theatre in Sloane Square opened in February 2000, with a policy still inspired by the first artistic director George Devine. The Royal Court is an international theatre for new plays and new playwrights, and the work shapes contemporary drama in Britain and overseas.

AWARDS FOR
THE ROYAL COURT

Jez Butterworth won the 1995 George Devine Award, the Writers' Guild New Writer of the Year Award, the Evening Standard Award for Most Promising Playwright and the Olivier Award for Best Comedy for Mojo.

The Royal Court was the overall winner of the 1995 Prudential Award for the Arts for creativity, excellence, innovation and accessibility. The Royal Court Theatre Upstairs won the 1995 Peter Brook Empty Space Award for innovation and excellence in theatre.

Michael Wynne won the 1996 Meyer-Whitworth Award for The Knocky. Martin McDonagh won the 1996 George Devine Award, the 1996 Writers' Guild Best Fringe Play Award, the 1996 Critics' Circle Award and the 1996 Evening Standard Award for Most Promising Playwright for The Beauty Queen of Leenane. Marina Carr won the 19th Susan Smith Blackburn Prize (1996/7) for Portia Coughlan. Conor McPherson won the 1997 George Devine Award, the 1997 Critics' Circle Award and the 1997 Evening Standard Award for Most Promising Playwright for The Weir. Ayub Khan-Din won the 1997 Writers' Guild Awards for Best West End Play and Writers' Guild New Writer of the Year and the 1996 John Whiting Award for East is East (co-production with Tamasha).

At the 1998 Tony Awards, Martin McDonagh's The Beauty Queen of Leenane (co-production with Druid Theatre Company) won four awards including Garry Hynes for Best Director and was nominated for a further two. Eugene Ionesco's The Chairs (co-production with Theatre de Complicite) was nominated for six Tony awards. David Hare won the 1998 Time Out Live Award for Outstanding Achievement and six awards in New York including the Drama League, Drama Desk and New York Critics Circle Award for Via Dolorosa. Sarah Kane won the 1998 Arts Foundation Fellowship in Playwriting. Rebecca Prichard won the 1998 Critics' Circle Award for Most Promising Playwright for Yard Gal (co-production with Clean Break).

Conor McPherson won the 1999 Olivier Award for Best New Play for The Weir. The Royal Court won the 1999 ITI Award for Excellence in International Theatre. Sarah Kane's Cleansed was judged Best Foreign Language Play in 1999 by Theater Heute in Germany. Gary Mitchell won the 1999 Pearson Best Play Award for Trust. Rebecca Gilman was joint winner of the 1999 George Devine Award and won the 1999 Evening Standard Award for Most Promising Playwright for The Glory of Living.

In 1999, the Royal Court won the European theatre prize New Theatrical Realities, presented at Taormina Arte in Sicily, for its efforts in recent years in discovering and producing the work of young British dramatists.

Roy Williams and Gary Mitchell were joint winners of the George Devine Award 2000 for Most Promising Playwright for Lift Off and The Force of Change respectively. At the Barclays Theatre Awards 2000 presented by the TMA, Richard Wilson won the Best Director Award for David Gieselmann's Mr Kolpert and Jeremy Herbert won the Best Designer Award for Sarah Kane's 4.48 Psychosis. Gary Mitchell won the Evening Standard's Charles Wintour Award 2000 for Most Promising Playwright for The Force of Change. Stephen Jeffreys' I Just Stopped by to See The Man won an AT&T: On Stage Award 2000.

David Eldridge's Under the Blue Sky won the Time Out Live Award 2001 for Best New Play in the West End. Leo Butler won the George Devine Award 2001 for Most Promising Playwright for Redundant. Roy Williams won the Evening Standard's Charles Wintour Award 2001 for Most Promising Playwright for Clubland. Grae Cleugh won the 2001 Olivier Award for Most Promising Playwright for Fucking Games. Richard Bean was joint winner of the George Devine Award 2002 for Most Promising Playwright for Under the Whaleback. Caryl Churchill won the 2002 Evening Standard Award for Best New Play for A Number. Vassily Sigarev won the 2002 Evening Standard Charles Wintour Award for Most Promising Playwright for Plasticine. Ian MacNeil won the 2002 Evening Standard Award for Best Design for A Number and Plasticine. Peter Gill won the 2002 Critics' Circle Award for Best New Play for The York Realist (English Touring Theatre).

ROYAL COURT BOOKSHOP

The bookshop offers a wide range of playtexts and theatre books, with over 1,000 titles. Located in the downstairs Bar and Food area, the bookshop is open Monday to Saturday, afternoons and evenings.

Many Royal Court playtexts are available for just £2 including works by Harold Pinter, Caryl Churchill, Rebecca Gilman, Martin Crimp, Sarah Kane, Conor McPherson, Ayub Khan-Din, Timberlake Wertenbaker and Roy Williams.

For information on titles and special events, Email: bookshop@royalcourttheatre.com
Tel: 020 7565 5024

PROGRAMME SUPPORTERS

The Royal Court (English Stage Company Ltd) receives its principal funding from London Arts. It is also supported financially by a wide range of private companies and public bodies and earns the remainder of its income from the box office and its own trading activities.
The Royal Borough of Kensington & Chelsea gives an annual grant to the Royal Court Young Writers' Programme.

The Jerwood Charitable Foundation continues to support new plays by new playwrights through the Jerwood New Playwrights series. Since 1993 A.S.K. Theater Projects of Los Angeles has funded a Playwrights' Programme at the theatre. Bloomberg Mondays, the Royal Court's reduced price ticket scheme, is supported by Bloomberg. Over the past seven years the BBC has supported the Gerald Chapman Fund for directors.

ROYAL COURT
JER WOOD THEATRE DOWNSTAIRS

6 - 30 August 2003
TOPDOG/ UNDERDOG

by **Suzan-Lori Parks**

Directed by George C. Wolfe

TOPDOG/UNDERDOG tells the story of two brothers, Lincoln and Booth. Their names, given to them as a joke, foretell a lifetime of sibling rivalry and resentment. Haunted by the past and their obsession with the street con Three Card Monte, the brothers are forced to confront the shattering reality of their future.

JERWOOD THEATRE UPSTAIRS

19 June - 12 July 2003
FOOD CHAIN

by **Mick Mahoney**

Directed by Anna Mackmin

Tony's doing well for himself, and his family. But what do you do when what you own is who you are?

Supported by Jerwood New Playwrights

Box Office 020 7565 5000
www.royalcourttheatre.co

JERWOOD
NEW PLAYWRIGHTS

Since 1993 Jerwood New Playwrights have contributed to some of the Royal Court's most successful productions, including SHOPPING AND FUCKING by Mark Ravenhill (co-production with Out of Joint), EAST IS EAST by Ayub Khan-Din (co-production with Tamasha), THE BEAUTY QUEEN OF LEENANE by Martin McDonagh (co-production with Druid Theatre Company), THE WEIR by Conor McPherson, REAL CLASSY AFFAIR by Nick Grosso, THE FORCE OF CHANGE by Gary Mitchell, ON RAFTERY'S HILL by Marina Carr (co-production with Druid Theatre Company), 4.48 PSYCHOSIS by Sarah Kane, UNDER THE BLUE SKY by David Eldridge, PRESENCE by David Harrower, HERONS by Simon Stephens, CLUBLAND by Roy Williams, REDUNDANT by Leo Butler, NIGHTINGALE AND CHASE by Zinnie Harris, FUCKING GAMES by Grae Cleugh, BEDBOUND by Enda Walsh, THE PEOPLE ARE FRIENDLY by Michael Wynne, OUTLYING ISLANDS by David Greig and IRON by Rona Munro. This season Jerwood New Playwrights are supporting UNDER THE WHALEBACK by Richard Bean, FLESH WOUND by Ché Walker, FALLOUT by Roy Williams and FOOD CHAIN by Mick Mahoney.

The Jerwood Charitable Foundation is a registered charity dedicated to imaginative and responsible funding and sponsorship of the arts, education, design and other areas of human endeavour and excellence.

HERONS by Simon Stephens
(photo: Pete Jones)

EAST IS EAST by Ayub Khan-Din
(photo: Robert Day)

CHÉ WALKER

Flesh Wound

ff

faber and faber

First published in 2003
by Faber and Faber Limited
3 Queen Square London WC1N 3AU
Published in the United States by Faber and Faber Inc.
an affiliate of Farrar, Straus and Giroux LLC, New York

Typeset by Country Setting, Kingsdown, Kent CT14 8ES
Printed in England by Mackays of Chatham plc, Chatham, Kent

A CIP record for this book
is available from the British Library

ISBN 0-571-22128-9

2 4 6 8 10 9 7 5 3 1

*The writer would like to thank the following
for their generous support and advice:*

Wilson Milam, Ian Rickson,
Graham Whybrow and Leah Schmidt

Characters

Joseph

Vincent

Deirdra

FLESH WOUND

We are on the top floor of Dalefoot Towers, a massive high-rise tower block in Somers Town, South Camden. The lights of the West End and beyond can be seen through the wide window. Below the block are the train tracks into Euston Station.

A low hum of passing traffic throughout.

The place is clean, but scruffy. Chipped plaster. Scuffed walls. Very sparse. A battered old sofa. Little kitchenette area with a sink and a hotplate. Door leads to bathroom. Small balcony overlooking the view.

The lights snap up on the following:

Deirdra in centre of room, her hand in her pocket.

Joseph, fifties, big guy, black overcoat, in the doorway, his hands turned palmways up towards Deirdra.

Deirdra I got a knife in my pocket and I killed people before.

Joseph I'm not taking one step inside your house till you invite me.

Deirdra I got ten rough brothers live in the block, be here in a flash, box you down all night, they like nothing better. All I gotta do is holler for 'em.

Joseph I've only come to be with your family in their hour of need.

Deirdra Stay there. Don't you even sway.

Joseph I'm not moving, love. Look. See? Still and calm, thass the way. (*Joseph lights a smoke.*)

Deirdra Oh, I'll get you a fuckin' ashtray, shall I? Who said you could smoke?

Joseph Your mother still live across the road?

Deirdra What?

Joseph Y'mum and me had our first night together up on the roof across the road.

Deirdra What?

Joseph I'm talking millions and millions of years ago.

Deirdra What you bringing my mum into this for?

Joseph We watched them detonate the old tenements that was here where your block is now. First charge went off, big cloud a' dust and then there loadsa these tramp people swarming out just squeezed into the cracks in the pavement. Your mum used to call them the Rat People, good way a' putting it, covered in fur they was. Next charge boom, your mum shook and I held her face. Third charge boom, just as I kissed her. Boom. And that was it. I was hooked on her, love. Y' mum told me it was her first time up there on the roof and I got no reason to disbelieve her. Any more.

Deirdra Thass all bollocks. Stop feeding me soup and fuck off.

Joseph walks to the window.

Oy. Cunt. You deaf?

Joseph I always knew the views would be magnificent up here. Twenty floors above the madness. You done well f' y'self, girl.

Deirdra You ain't s'posed to be in the flat. You s'posed to be by the door. Don't take the piss outta me, I'll have you shot.

Joseph leans over the balcony a little gingerly.

Joseph That traffic must get on your tits after a bit, dunnit? 'S got much worse since I was with your mum across the road.

Deirdra Whadjuh mean, with my mum across the road? You keep dropping that in. Whadjuh mean?

Joseph Bit . . . well, a bit galling, really. Everybody streaming through to get up West. I don't reckon they know we're here at all, do you? Only time anyone notices us is when a young fella gets hisself murdered round here. Then there's a great hue and a cry and a beating of breasts . . . and then fuck all. (*Joseph takes off his coat.*)

Deirdra I never said nutting about you taking off your coat. Want me to call up my brothers? I will, y' know.

Joseph folds coat neatly over chair.

Joseph When me and your mum was younger, a fella jumped off a . . . whassit called, the big block down that way, Holmrook Flats. Old boy he was, string vest, electric blue Y-fronts, sometimes see him in Jitou's shop scratchin' his balls and mutterin' 'bout he's a war veteran, he's a war veteran, banging on about his medals, bit a' local colour, pay no mind, landed right in fronta where they got the laundrette sign. Looked like a bottla broken cough syrup. Two jets a' blood out each ear about eight foot either direction. They come and took his body away. But they left his blood. Your old dear's on the blower to the council wailing about it, like thass gonna do anything, finally she took it on herself and rounded up a lotta other women from the vicinity, they all go out with the buckets and the brushes, got down on their hands and knees and they scrubbed and they scrubbed and they scrubbed. Till sunset. The other women said, 'Look we gotta go, we got teas to prepare,' but your mum . . . your mum kept on at it. Alone. She was possessed. Took her a lotta graft, that did. But it was clean. Coulda ate my dinner off that pavement at the death of it. Admire her for it, Deirdra. She thought it was wrong. She went out and fixed it. Eyes flashing juss like yourn, my dear.

Joseph takes a seat.

Deirdra You're getin a li'l free and easy with my flat. You ain't staying, y'know. Y'ain't stayin and I ain't afraid.

Joseph 'Course she had her unreasonable side, your mum. I can see that in you and all, my love. Lemme tell you 'boutcha old dear . . . I'm drinking in the Eastnor Castle, right, this little barmaid pinches my ass at closing time and then winks at me, li'l spunky redhead thing she was, I didn't think a great deal of it, li'l bit too bladdered to be honest, but somehow your mum catches a whiff of it, like she always did, don't ask me how, clairvoyant is my guess, I ain't even finished my drink and your mum's coming through the door, sez, 'Where's the slag been showing out to my husban'?' Sees the barmaid, no further questions, your honour, drags this girl out, hammers her into the pavement. Battered her. Closed up both her eyes, your mum did. Botha them. Then she sez to her, 'How you gonna wink at someone else's husband now? Slut.' (*Beat.*) I love your mother.

Deirdra Dunno how you got hold a' that story, but you're lying. Mum told me that story but the man involved was her first husband and he's now dearly departed.

Joseph Your mum told you I was dearly departed?

Deirdra Dead as a doornail.

Joseph Whatcha mum told you wasn't truthful, darling.

Deirdra Shut up. And when did your ballbag grow so big you could call me darling?

Joseph I'm not dead, love. Never been so alive.

Deirdra You're delusional.

Joseph S'pose thass what I deserve. To be erased like this.

Deirdra You're some sorta fantasist. You and my mum, thass disgusting . . . My mum wouldn't have fuck-all to do with you.

Joseph Oh, my dear . . . She had everything to do with me. Everything.

Deirdra If my dad was still here, he'd rip your throat out for talking about my mum like that.

Joseph I was your dad's only friend round here. Have a guess where I met him, go on.

Deirdra I ain't guessin fuck-all.

Joseph I met him on my first day working on this very block we're in now. No one else liked him, but I took to him straight away. Never worked so hard in all our lives. Put us both off straight work, it did.

Deirdra You never worked on this block.

Joseph But it does feel a little bit special coming up here and knowing people have made their home in it over the last forty-odd year. My sweat is keeping this building upright, love.

Deirdra You never did fuck-all like that. I can tell from the coat.

Joseph He he . . . Ladies always struck on the cut of my coat. This coat is peculiar to Burberry's, doncha know?

Deirdra You look like a tramp.

Joseph Put on a lotta size working on this block, your mother was pleased.

Deirdra Shut up.

Joseph One evening when we're down deep hacking away at the crust, a nice Bentley rolls up, coupla fellas plainly up to no good go over to the foreman and shoot him a look that . . . that warps the fabric of time, so he slopes off, burns a quick tab. The fellas come up to me and your dad press some cash in our palms and ask us to do some extra shovelling for 'em. Me and your old man are fine with the cash and agree. These fellas go to the boot of the Bentley, pull out an Afghan rug, pair of feet stickin' out one end, one shoe on, the other juss a sock . . . they hurl it down into the pit. Big dust cloud swirls up, juss missed your old man. He says, 'Hey, what you doing?' But I tell him shush, and the fellas says there's more money if we take care of it properly for 'em. We didn't say another word, juss started shovelling. That was how me and your old man got started. That was our first adventure in the shadows.

Deirdra My old man would never associate with the likes of you.

Joseph It was me introduced him to your old dear. Bit of a mistake in retrospect. Had to watch 'em fall in love. There's a sweetness to even that. Two people I loved very much . . .

Deirdra I don't appreciate you coming up here and telling lies 'bout my mum and dad, my mum and dad were righteous hard-working people from round here. You don't know my mum. You never knew my dad. And you don't know me. I tell you for the last time. Fuck off out of it, cuntox.

Joseph I can believe this is hard. But it is the truth.

Deirdra Mum was very specific. You're dead.

Joseph I can understand them telling you that. I have not been someone you'd wanna be related to. Probably the best thing they coulda toldjuh.

Deirdra You died when you fell in the canal after a binge. You floated all the way up to Mile End before they fished you out. Mum had to go down and identify your body. She said you stank.

Joseph Heh. There is a grain of truth in that. I did like walking down the canal because I could sing under the bridges, bit a doo-wop, some a the old Irish songs . . . And I was drunk. That much is definitely true. But what happened was, this coupla Kentish Town boys come out a' nowhere and set upon me. Fought 'em off as best I could, but they stabbed me several times, around eight, I think, have a look, girl, go on.

Joseph lifts up his shirt to reveal eight knife scars on his belly.

Deirdra I don't wanna look at that. Fuckin' put that away.

Joseph Thing about being stabbed is you don't feel it, just your ears start to ring very loudly, tells you we have to get away from this pain and my body dives into the canal, completely fucks the mohair I'm wearing, so now I'm in the water and I'm safe, right? But the problem is, the other side of the canal is just wall, there's no towpath, so they're waiting for me, baying for my blood, and I have to swim for absolute miles, hit a point where I coulda gone under, coulda juss surrendered to it, but what pulled me through was Vincent.

Deirdra Whadjuh mean, Vincent?

Joseph I thought I could see him swimming just in fronta me in the murk, he'd a been roughly eight, and I managed to catch on his feet and he pulled me along, laughing all the way, he was.

Kentish Town boys got bored after a few miles, gimme up for dead. And they were very nearly right 'cause my cuts have got infected from all the rat's piss in that water and God knows what else, I was touch and go for a few days, delirious, vomiting up all sorts.

Deirdra Don't tell lies about my Vincent. Thass my family. Whatever else he is, thass my family.

Joseph When they was pumping the filth out my lungs, I was in a very bad condition for days. Your mum took to the rosary beads like a born nun, chanting away in the back, I used to wake up to it and then slip back under. Took credit for my recovery. Power of prayer, she reckoned. But your mum couldn't bear to be near me once I got better. Never touched me again. Granted, the bilge had got into my skin and I smelled ferocious. Even Vincent was shy of me. So in a sense, she told you the truth. I did die in that canal. At least for her, I did.

Pause.

Deirdra Whatchou get jooked for?

Joseph Summink I was alleged to have said coming out the Delhi Diner one night, just a loada Chinese whispers.

Deirdra This is all a lie. You died, then she met my dad and they was courtin' and he made it alright for a while. Vincent even called him daddy.

Joseph Where is Vincent?

Deirdra Vincent who?

Joseph Don't be silly, love. Vincent your mother's son. Vincent your only brother.

Deirdra He's in the Bahamas.

Joseph I come to help him. Where is he?

Deirdra County Durham.

Joseph I'm his lifeline.

Deirdra Shut up.

Joseph I'm his father.

Deirdra You're a liar.

Joseph Vincent is my little boy.

Deirdra Bollox.

Joseph I come here because my boy is in trouble and I wanna help him.

Deirdra Howjuh know your boy is in trouble?

Joseph You a parent? When you're a parent, you'll understand. You juss get a feeling. Your child is in trouble. They need their father. You get a feeling and you come to where your child is.

Deirdra You're one a' Rosie Calderazzo's brothers, juss one I ain't seen before, thass all, they've sent you up here to sniff around for Vincent, go and check the half-sister lives on her jax top a' the tower block, she'll tell you anything you wanna know, they're only half related, she ain't got no loyalty, then we can find the boy and slicey-slicey oncey-twicey, what, you think I'm some kinda cunt? Think I juss fuckin moved here from back a' bush or summink? You fake. You poodle. Tell me another lie about my poor mother again and see what I do to you, 'cause I ain't fraida no washed out cardboard donkey like you, y'get me?

Joseph You move like her . . . You sound like her . . . You even smell like her.

Deirdra Stop telling me I look like my mother, thass the typa rudeness I takes umbrage to very quick, I DON'T LOOK NOTHING LIKE MY MOTHER!

Pause.

Joseph I seen you when you was a li'l kid once, had your hair in bunches.
Your dad was pushing you on the swings.

Deirdra You don't know my dad. My dad's a decent man.

Joseph The next time I saw you, you was in your teens. Beating seven shades a' shit outa Vincent on Royal College Street. I love my boy like the sun coming up, but he's not a fighter, is he? Not like you. You were unstoppable. Clawed him. Pummelled him. It was a true rage. You were your old dear all over again and it was wonderful to watch. God help me, but it was.

Deirdra Whatchou doin', watchin' me all these years?

Joseph Wanting to be a part of it.

Deirdra I never seen you before in my life.

Joseph Thass something thass wrong, Deirdra.

Joseph lights another smoke. Offers one to Deirdra, who declines.

Why you had to hit him? What had he done you that time?

Pause.

Deirdra I beat Vincent up on Royal College Street because he told that boy Phivos Thoupou I fancied him. Thass why I punched him that time. Still had my braces. I think thass the fight you woulda seen. Bust his lip wide open with my sovereign ring.

Joseph Didjou fancy that boy Phivos Thoupou?

Deirdra Thass none of your business who I fancy.

Pause.

Joseph Whass he like? Vincent. Is he a nice man?

Deirdra does not answer.

I really need to know.

Deirdra Havin' Vincent for a brother is like having a chicken bone stuck in your throat.

Joseph He's in trouble.

Deirdra Vincent is always in trouble.

Joseph But this time you're worried.

Deirdra Not unduly.

Joseph No, no. This time is different because I felt it and had to come down here.

Deirdra Bollocks.

Joseph You know it's true. And you know who I am.

Deirdra Yeah? So where you been, then?

Joseph I been scared is where I been.

Pause.

Deirdra Mum said Vincent's father was a handsome fella.

Joseph Maybe I was once.

Deirdra Said you could charm the birds outa the trees.

Joseph Whass she say about Vincent?

Deirdra She sez she's washed her hands of him, but I don't believe her. Nobody ever washes their hands of Vincent.

Joseph She washed her hands of me.

Deirdra Don't fuckin' blame her, from the state a' you.

Joseph You gonna let me help him?

Deirdra doesn't answer. Joseph looks out of the window.

Only time anyone notices us is when a young fella gets hisself murdered round here. Then there's a great hue and a cry and a beating of breasts . . . And then fuck-all. (*Beat.*) Rosie Calderazzo . . . Who is she?

Deirdra Big girl, busted hip, got a limp, Coke bottle spex. I see her in the park eating dirt a coupla times. She's like . . . I dunno whatchour s'posed to say, like, . . . retarded or backwards or summink. Always looks to me like she's got the raving hump. Talks to herself. Scolds herself off, then answers herself with some backchat, I don't know what the fuck goes on with her. But you know what? . . . I catch her face one time outside the laundrette, she's juss placid, staring into space . . . And she looked very beautiful. Very beautiful.

Joseph And this girl's got a problem with Vincent?

Deirdra Vincent ain't exactly been a pillar of the community. Done a lotta slacknesses round this vicinity in recent memory. Lotta people wouldn't shed one tear if he's gone. To be honest, lotta people breathe a sigh of fuckin' relief if the Calderazzos just kill him.

Joseph Whass their grievance with Vincent?

Deirdra Fucked if I know. Could be anything.

Joseph You ain't all that bothered, looks to me.

Deirdra I'm bothered. Course I'm bothered. He's blood to me. But Vincent don't lissen. He doesn't see what the problem is. He thinks iss all a comedy. Me and Mum been telling him for years about hisself and he juss laughs at us. After a while, s'like havin an elderly relative.

Joseph How's that?

Deirdra You know the phone call is coming. You know they're not long for this world. Juss prepare y'self as best you can.

Joseph I gotta find him.

Deirdra You ain't Vincent's dad. Nah.

Joseph Look at my face. Properly. No, look at it. Look how deep-set my eyes are. Don't recognise? Come closer, dear.

She doesn't come to him.

Darling, I'm no threat to you. Look at me. You can see that I mean you well.

She still doesn't come.

Shy one, eh? Wanna make me work for it? Alright . . .

Pause.

Look at the top of my head. (*He bends his head so she can see.*) Can you see the ridge there? Can you see it?

Pause.

No, you have to touch it. No way around it, I'm afraid.

Pause.

For you to know who I am, you're gonna have to rest your hand on top my bonce.

Pause.

Deirdra This where you switch on me?

Joseph No, love. This is where you put your hand on my bonce.

Pause.

I'm not bad news. Not for you.

Pause.

Deirdra Get on your knees.

Joseph What?

Deirdra I have to feel safe.

> *Joseph laboriously gets down on his hands and knees,*
> *groaning and grunting excessively with the effort.*
> *Deirdra pulls out a large kitchen knife from the*
> *kitchenette.*

Joseph Y'not gonna fuckin' execute me, are you, love?

Deirdra Just a precaution. (*Deirdra moves closer. She*
stretches out a hand.)

Joseph Thass it, girl, lovely.

> *She puts her hand out timorously.*

I'm gonna put my hand on your hand so you can feel
what I want you to feel.

Deirdra You try any tricks and I'll stab you right
through your fuckin' eyeball, so help me God.

Joseph Well, I definitely don't want that now, do I, love?
(*Joseph takes her hand and places it on the top of his*
head.) Feel that ridge? Thass it. Juss there . . . You know
who's got a ridge like that, doncha?
Thass Vincent's ridge. And my ridge. And my grandad's
ridge. And my dead brother's ridge, properly dead, not
like I'm s'posed to be but really and truly dead in the
harshest sense of the word. (*Beat.*) You feel it, doncha?
I can see in your face you can feel it.

> *Pause.*

Deirdra She told us y'name was Joseph.

Joseph Thass right, love. My name is Joseph.

Deirdra Why she turn from you?

Pause.

Joseph Weren't like one awful thing I done. It was more like Chinese water torture. Drip, drip. Injustice. Little comments. Not coming home. Juss built up over the years and she had to turn away. A blind man could see I was gonna lose her. And my Vincent. My little fella.

A commotion outside.
    Deirdra and Joseph leap to their feet.

Vincent (*offstage*) Deirdra! Lemme in, sistren! Wanna give you a cuddle!

Joseph Is that him?

Deirdra Knew he'd come here eventually.

Joseph He's here!

Deirdra You wanted to meet him.

Joseph I'm not ready.

Vincent (*offstage*) Nobody home? Deirdra? Juss the micey-wicey in there?

Sound of Vincent fiddling with the lock.

Joseph I can't.

Deirdra No way out, darling, we're on the top floor.

Joseph hides in the little bathroom.

What you doing? Stay and meet with him! 'S what you're here for, isn't it?

Joseph shuts the door.

Joseph!

The door swings open and Vincent enters.

Vincent How many fuckin' children did Mrs Calderazzo deliver? I juss been pursued through King's Cross all the way to here, through Charrington Street, Ossulton Street, all the streets, they're patrolling around in these massive Mitsubishi Shogun open-top jeeps, I'm dipping through the corners, but then as I'm coming down by William Collins my back get a chill, look behind me, six of the brothers right up my arsehole, I turn round and there's six more brothers in fronta me, so I start to twist and run, duck down a side street, hide myself in one a' them old-fashioned phone boxes, pretend to make a call, reckon nobody's gonna see me in there, but of course they sight me straight away and you know the really big one, Arnold, the veteran, Arnold's leading the charge, but I've wedged the door shut with this sharp stick I been carrying for lockpicking, and I reckon I must be safe, but Arnold juss cocks back his left fist all the way back to fuckin' Holloway, hauls off and lets it fly KAPOW! The fuckin' booth is at a tilt, Deirdra, swear to God, and Arnold hauls the left back again and BLAM! Fucking dents right through the door, the whole phone booth lets out this, like, tired groan, sounds like Mum . . . and it ends up on iss side, so now I'm trapped in this upended phone booth, Arnold's suckin' the broken glass out of his knuckles, he sez finish it, the younger brothers moving in now, I can see the machetes come out the long coats, and I'm thinking this is it, the final flatline, and I get all calm, like, accepting, like, juss for a second, and then this supersonic energy kicks in, I got this whooosh sound in my ears, I'm wriggling kicking scrabbling, somehow I manage to get away from them and duss up to here, but I tell you this: Mrs Calderazzo must have a womb like half an old grapefruit after pushing out all them babies, truss me.

*During the above Vincent has helped himself to a
large drink of rum, found Deirdra's fags stuffed down
the side of the sofa.*

You got anything to eat, Deirdra? I'm so hungry I could
eat Christ off the cross. (*He flops down on the sofa.*)

Deirdra They never followed you here, did they? I can
do without them griefing up my drum.

Vincent They won't come up here. You've tucked y'self
away up here so quiet, none a' them even know I got a
sister.

Deirdra Best be right, Vincent. Calderazzo trouble is
trouble in depth.

Vincent Lemme stay here for a li'l while, catch my
breath, sistren. Come on . . .

Deirdra Whyncha go and stay with Mum?

Vincent Mum still claiming she never bear me.
   Mum sez she don't have no son, and that I don't exist.
Last time she tells me I'm the reason for the pills.

Deirdra Fuckin' pills, fuckin' pills, spend my life tryin'a
get hold a' them fuckin' pills for her. Juhknow she faked
a prescription and got turfed outa Boots last week like a
homeless?

Vincent Toldjuh before, lemme get 'em. Cheaper.

Deirdra Yeah? And when you don't turn up with 'em,
who gets the three o'clock phone call with the tears and
the sweats? Certainly not you.

Vincent Mum won't let me do anything for her, you
know that. Called me a thief last time.

Deirdra You are a thief. I know you snatched Millie
Brown's purse last time you was up in The Palace. She's

dancin' round, sees you and somebody sounds like Mishak running through the fire exit and her purse is gone.

Vincent Never heard a' Millie Brown and I don't know fuck-all about no purse.

Deirdra She's Mum's social worker. Recognised you off the photo on the mantelpiece.

Vincent Bollocks. Bitch lies like the police.

Deirdra Everyone's lying about poor li'l Vincent. Rosie Calderazzo lyin' and all?

Vincent Thass not fair. I been calumniated and you know it.

Deirdra Them brothers of hers are pretty sure about the whole matter.

Vincent They're juss judgin' me on past shenanigans. Juss 'cause I done some li'l like slacknesses in the distant past, they can't accept that I've changed and moved on, Sis. You know that. All the people who know me know that.

Deirdra All the people who know you know that where you're concerned, nothing ever changes and no progress is ever made.

Vincent Giss a cup a tea, cutiepie.

Deirdra You smell unpleasant, Vincent.

Vincent It's the fear.

Deirdra You're stinking out my fuckin' sofa. Get up.

Vincent gets up.

Vincent Toljuh not to take the plastic off it.

Deirdra is on the sofa with a sponge, maniacally scrubbing where Vincent was.

Thass it. Erase my presence. No one in this family wants to admit I exist. Got any idea what that does to a fella? Warps him, thass what it does. I coulda been a violinist if it wasn't for you and Mum.

Deirdra Shut up.

Vincent I need to change my clothes. Started to offend myself how I smell.

Deirdra Someone in there.

Vincent No . . . You got a visitor? My li'l sis got a visitor? Whass the occasion? You ain't had sex in well over a decade. Who is he? Or she? They local? Lissen to your bigger brother, don't take no shit from no man. You're a prize, Deirdra, truss me you're a prize.

Deirdra Joseph. Come out here and meet Vincent.

Vincent Joseph. Thass a nice name. Do I know him?

Joseph enters.

Joseph Nice to see you again, Vincent.

Vincent Whozzis?

Deirdra This is Joseph.

Joseph Heard you was in a bit a' bother.

Vincent Whozzis?

Deirdra Vincent . . .

Joseph I know it ain't easy, son. Ain't easy for any of us.

Vincent Shut up. Whozzis?

Deirdra You know full well who it is.

Joseph I want to help you, Vincent.

Vincent Shut up. Whozzis?

Joseph Vincent . . .

Deirdra Joseph wants to help you get it together,
Vincent.

Vincent DON'T TALK TO ME LIKE I'M AN IDIOT!
This man is not supposed to be here. This man is a snake
in the grass. Aren't ya? This man is a Calderazzo. You
shtuppid mug.

Joseph V –

Vincent Shut up! Ainchou got any nous? They fuckin'
sniffed you out. How could you not read this one? He's
an enemy. Doncha see the resemblance? He's another
Calderazzo brother come to fuck me up. Look at him.

Deirdra No, he's –

Vincent Lied to you, whass he toldjuh? That I know him
somehow? That we're related in some fashion? (*to
Joseph*) YOU AND ME ARE NOT RELATED! I don't
know you.

Joseph Vincent, I –

Vincent No words! No words out your mouth. Ever
again. You done a good job with my sis 'cause she
doesn't move in this world, she don't always read things
correctly, thass why I love her, 'cause she's pure, but you
ain't lying to me, so shut your hole, don't even make a
fart noise till I tell you you can.

Joseph I know you're angry, I –

> *Vincent pulls out a gun from under Deirdra's sofa and
> pistol-whips Joseph once across the face.*

Vincent Who's angry? Eh? Who here in this room is
feeling angry?
I'm not angry! I ain't angry at all. I'm the opposite of
angry, which is intelligent. Don't confuse the two again.
Never mistake my intelligence for anger, Joseph.

Deirdra Whassat gun doing under my couch?

Vincent Been storing it there for a while.

Joseph Vincent, I –

Vincent Get on the floor.

Deirdra Who give you the gun?

Joseph I dunno if I can, I got terrible sciatica, son –

Vincent DON'T CALL ME SON! Get on the floor. Ain't arsking again.

> *Pause.*
>> *Joseph gets on the floor.*

Deirdra Who give you the gun?

Vincent Nobody gimme the gun, Mishak sold me the gun last time he was round.

Deirdra Last time he was round? Whadjuh mean, last time he was round?

Vincent Last time we stocked a loada stuff in your drum, girl.

Deirdra You been using my place as a warehouse?

Joseph My back's fucked, Vincent, I –

Vincent You speak when you're fuckin' spoken to and not before! More than a warehouse, love. We both needed to spit-roast a coupla slags, nobody knows you round here, no one thinks we're related, and you had absolutely no idea till juss now that anything was amiss, so whass the problem? Don't make a scene, eh, girl? 'S unbecoming.

Deirdra How could you bring Mishak McCormack into my home?

Vincent Mishak's my friend. Been more loyal than this fuckin' family ever have.

Joseph My back really is terrible, Vincent, please –

Vincent Shut up. Your last minutes on earth, this how you wanna spend them? Whining aboutcha back spasms?

Joseph Don't do this, Vincent, you're better than this . . .

Deirdra Vincent, I really think you're being a little exuberant about this.

Vincent Whadjuh do with that plastic for the sofa?

Deirdra Threw it away.

Vincent Bollocks. Toldjuh to hold on to that. Get the shower curtain out the bath.

Deirdra This is torture you're creating for y'self, Vincent.

Vincent Nah. This is me putting a few things right. Tired a' getting chased through Somers. Get the shower curtain.

> *Pause.*
> *Deirdra goes into the bathroom.*
> *Vincent lights up a smoke.*

Wanna fag?

Joseph Very much so.

Vincent Tough titty. None spare.

> *Deirdra comes back out with the shower curtain.*

Here y'are, skippy. Whadjuh call y'self? Joseph. Thass a laugh. Go on, Joseph, wrap y'self up in that, mate, there's a good fella.

Joseph Can't we at least listen to each other, son?

Vincent Call me son again and it ain't gonna be pretty. Get in that wrap. Come on, get in it.

   Joseph wraps himself up in the shower curtain.

Thass it. Look like a Roman. Palermo, innit, the Calderazzos?

Joseph I'm from Somers Town two generations.

Vincent Shut up. You ain't from anywhere near here. Stand up.

   Joseph stands up.

Go over to the window.

   Joseph goes over to the window.

Open it up.

   Joseph opens the window.
      Sounds of traffic, trains.
      Rush of cold air into the room.

Deirdra Come on, Vincent, I got a say in this, this is my place and I don't deserve what you got planned.

   Joseph starts tiptoeing to door.

Vincent Ain't happening to you, iss happening to him and iss too late to stop me 'cause I'm on a roll. Time to flip the script. Enough of being victimised by that fuckin' family. 'S the only way to deal with these Calderazzos.

   Joseph still creeping.
      Vincent raises the gun at him.

Oy. Twinkletoes. Look at me. Two options. Jump out the window. Or get shot in the eye. Then get thrown out. Whass your preference?

Deirdra Don't, Vincent, please, He's only tryin'a put things right.

Vincent Thass exactly what we're gonna do. Put things right. (*to Joseph*) Come on, mate. Whass it gonna be? One in the eye? Or freedom? You won't survive the drop, but what a rush. What a view. Pure freedom for five seconds. Pack up your cares and woes, there you go, there you go, winging low. Come on, soldier, whass it gonna be? Ain't got all day, got fish to fry and kites to fly, whass your final answer?

Deirdra This man is your blood, Vincent.

Vincent See? Done a good job, didncha? She believes you. But Deirdra's soppy like that. Incha, D? Lovely girl, really, heart a gold, doncha think?

Joseph I want you to shoot me.

Deirdra Don't do this, Vincent . . .

Vincent Very good. Very good. I like this man. Very good. Wants to go, be set on the road to glory by little Vincent. Wants my face to be the last thing he sees.

> *Joseph crawls to Vincent.*
> *He places his forehead against the end of his gun.*

Joseph I do want your face to be the last thing I see, you're right. Been tryin'a imagine . . . Would you know me if you saw me? If you saw me and you knew me, what would you want from me? In my fantasy, we talk and talk for days about ev'rything till we juss cry in each other's arms, and we have the cuddle I been storing for you for twenty years. But I made myself a big promise. The promise was this. I would abide by whatever you decided to do about me. Irregardless of my own feelings. No complaints. I'm juss glad I got to meet you once again before I die. And I'm very glad you got such a lovely sister who loves you so much. She fights with you, but she has such love for you, son. Thass all. S'pose I shouldna come, but I still feel right that I did. I sought

32

you out and tried to say I'm sorry. So just get it done, son. I love you and I'm tired and I want you to just get it done.

Vincent pulls the trigger.
Click.
Empty.
Pause.

Vincent That fucking Mishak McCormack . . .

Deirdra He's skanked you, innhe?

Vincent Shut up.

Joseph Am I dead?

Vincent Yes.

Joseph Is this dead?

Vincent Yes.

Deirdra Dunno why you have him for a friend, Vincent.

Vincent Thass it. The Calderazzos are gonna skewer me.

Joseph I think I've had a little accident.

Deirdra All the help you've given Mishak over the years, he should juss be giving you a gun, not selling you one. How much money did you give Mishak for this piece?

Vincent It was a very reasonable rate.

Deirdra But bullets are extra.

Vincent You got any? 'Cause if you haven't, juss be quiet because thass what I need at this moment in time.

Deirdra No, I don't have bullets, I'm normal, Vincent. Bullets are not normal. Bullets are a sign that your life has taken a downward turn.

Joseph I'd like to go to the toilet and clean myself up if that's alright with you both.

Vincent It's not alright with us both. You stay there and sit in your own piss. (*to Deirdra*) And you're gonna go to Mishak and get the ammo for this piece.

Deirdra Absolutely no chance. No chance, Vincent. You're mad.

Vincent You know I can't go. They got Range Rovers and Mitsubishi Shoguns.

Deirdra Nope. This is your stink. Breathe it in and learn to love it.

Vincent You don't do it, I'm gonna batter you.

Deirdra You ain't beaten me in a fight since I was nine.

He points the gun at her.

You got no bullets. Worst you can do is throw it at me.

Vincent Bollocks. You're irritating me, Deirdra.

Deirdra You're irritating me. You're in my house with your madness. I'm the one who's being imposed on, not you. I'm not the problem, you're the problem, all this is happening 'cause a' y'self, nobody toldjuh to go messing with that poor girl, nobody toldjuh to alienate the whole fucking community by being a thieving piss-taking little slack cunt so you got no one to turn to and definitely nobody toldjuh to come round to my drum and try and shoot your estranged father, in fact, not being funny right, bruv, but JUST WHAT IN THE FUCK DO YOU TAKE ME FOR?

Vincent He's not my father, he's a Calderazzo. They're sly, that lot.

Deirdra I'm not the problem.

Vincent Get me the bullets. If you do it, I'll change completely.

Deirdra laughs.

If I get carved up and dropped in the canal, then you'll never know if I had the strength. Mum won't have the chance to see her boy improve. You gonna look Mum in the eye when she arsk you if I ever said I was gonna change?

Pause.

Deirdra You're a fuckin' asshole, Vincent . . .

Vincent scrabbles around in his pocket for some money.

You gotta pay him and all?

Vincent No point in going up to the Cross and having to come back 'cause Mishak feels like being an obstreperous cunt for a day. (*He hands her the money.*)

Deirdra Still the same place?

Vincent Still the same place. Push the buzzer with a pen.

Deirdra Faulty wires?

Vincent Covered in phlegm.

Deirdra puts on her coat.

Deirdra This is the last time, Vee.

Vincent I love you.

She turns to go.

Joseph I enjoyed our talk.

She leaves.
Pause.

She's such good news, that girl.

Vincent looks out of the window.

Vincent How comes you never took the drop? No guarantee a bullet's gonna kill you straight away. You could linger for hours.

Joseph Got you some presents in my pocket.

Vincent Don't want 'em.

Joseph struggles in the plastic and fishes out a crumpled bag.

Joseph Here y'are, son.

Vincent Toljuh already 'bout calling me son. I ain't your son. I'm a stranger.

Joseph fishes in his bag and comes out with a pair of Spiderman Y-fronts, way too small, to fit a child of eight.

Joseph Look. See? (*Sings.*)
Spiderman . . . Spiderman . . .
Does whatever a spider can . . .
Is he strong? Lissen, bud . . .
He's got radioactive blood,
Look out . . .
Here comes the Spiderman . . .

Vincent Stop singing.

Joseph I'm upset to see you this way.

Vincent I'm upset to see you at all.

Joseph At least take the present.

Vincent Don't fit.

Joseph Course iss gonna fit.

Vincent It don't fit, look at it, thass a child's size and I'm not a child.

Pause.

Joseph You love spiderman . . .

*He looks at the Y-fronts. Realises they couldn't
possibly fit.*

There are other presents in my pocket.

Vincent Don't want 'em.

Joseph I'm juss tryin'a . . . Just . . .

Vincent I know what you're juss tryin'a . . . just. Begged
Mum to get me them pants, but she wouldn't budge,
reckoned they were ungodly. But buying me a pair of
underpants don't make you my dad.

Joseph Stop pretending you don't recognise me and less
have a conversation, eh? All I wanna do is help you get
out of this trouble.

Vincent You got bullets for this gun?

Joseph No.

Vincent Then you can't help.

Joseph There's other ways, Vincent. Doesn't have to be
bloodshed.

Vincent Thass all there is left now. You know that as well
as I do. Nothing but savagery. Calderazzos run Somers.
Once she comes back with my bullets, I'm gonna get in a
car and drive somewhere pretty like Margate.

Joseph Whatever you've done . . . We can go and we
can talk to them about it. I got a little weight. Not
much, but I'm a veteran. That's gonna get me a fair
hearing, they have to gimme that after the stuff I done
round here.

Vincent Too late, mate. The fatwah has been pronounced.

37

Joseph Gimme a chance to fix it. The Calderazzos musta heard a' me.

Vincent Give it up. Stop the charade.

Joseph Why they after you? You done summink to the li'l backwards girl?

Vincent She's not a backwards. She just a li'l slow in her thinking. And she's not a li'l girl. She's my age, near enough.

Joseph You done summink to her?

Vincent They say I have. But I haven't.

Joseph So for them iss a clan thing. And iss happened on their doorstep. Tricky. Needs tact. You got any dough to speak of, Vincent?

Vincent Do I look like I got any dough to speak of?

Joseph Thass alright, I got a little scratch I could let you hold. The trick is not to seem like you're tryin'a buy your way out of it, that iss a sign of how seriously you take your mistake, and how much regard you have for them.

Vincent Ain't made no mistake, have I? Picked my name out of a hat.

Joseph No smoke without fire, Vincent.

Vincent Shut up.

Joseph Even if you never done this one, you done summink along the way thass brought you to their attention.

Vincent Ain't done fuck-all. Spent my life not getting too big for my boots round here, worke out my own level a' snide behaviour years ago and I never overstep. I don't want nothing to do with the heavyweight firms like the Calderazzos. They kill a man on Friday on the High

Street and come Monday they're in Malaysia running a fuckin' wine bar. Thass not me. I don't want fuck-all to do with that. I'm a piss-taker, not an assassin. But I'm not going to die at anyone else's hands but my own. Thass an imposition that I won't accept. Might have to move outa Camden, but thass fine. Gone downhill round here, anyways.

Joseph If you knew how this cuts me, Vincent.

Vincent Ain't for you to be getting cut about me.

Joseph You were the most beautifullest boy in the whole world, you were. I'd give anything for you to look at me the way you used to when I put you to bed. Your mum could never get you off to sleep. You'd cry and she'd fall apart. It was always me that calmed you down. It was me. Not her. Me. Nobody except me. She never had the knack. The knack was your earhole. Just the outer shell. If you stroked it lightly enough and slowly enough, you'd stop crying. Then the inner shell. Circular motion, gettin' all the swirls. You'd yawn a few times, then you'd be gone. Into the Land of Nod. Your mum hated that I could do it. She saw it as some sorta reproach. But I never told her the magic spot. (*Joseph reaches out and touches his ear, stroking it.*) Thass the spot. Juss there. Hasn't changed . . . Hasn't changed . . . Thass the one . . .

Vincent You better take your fuckin' hand off my ear straight away.

Joseph moves his hand up his head.

Joseph And there's the ridge.

Vincent What fuckin' ridge?

Joseph Gimme your hand. (*Joseph takes Vincent's hand and puts it on his head.*) Feel that? Thass family, that is.

We all got it. Thass our stamp. Your grandad had it. My brother had it. We all got it.

Vincent Stop touching my head and stop talking to me altogether.

Joseph When I was young, I thought I'd cracked my head open and thass what it was, spent mosta my youth tryin'a recall when I banged my head so hard it formed this ridge, but one day I was wrestling about with your grandad and I got hold of his head, I was gonna bite it, and I realised that he had the same landscape on his head. Remarkable, isn't it? Like a cliff. Touch my one, son. (*Joseph puts his hand on Vincent's, guiding him along his head.*) See? They're the same. Our skulls are the same.

Vincent You look like a Calderazzo . . .

Joseph I'm not a Calderazzo, son. I'm your daddy come home to keep you safe.

   Vincent sags a little. Sings, to the tune of 'A Bushel and a Peck'.

   I love you . . .
   A pickle and a poo . . .
   Bet your bottom dollar I do . . .

Vincent Stop it . . . You're bad . . .

Joseph I know I been bad. But I'm here now and I'm puttin' it right. There it is. You see? Nothing is ever gonna get in our way again, kiddo.

Vincent Don't say that . . .

Joseph No, I'm very serious. Know why? Because I'm very clear. The clarity has been hard-won, but it is here and it's set me free. My most recent incarceration, first day in,skip onto the landing for a game a' ping pong and this fella's coming up, name a' John, from the Hornchurch I think he was, he stops bang in fronta me, tells me step aside. Now this sorta thing on the pavement, iss nothing, no meaning, but on the inside . . . The first fight you're offered inside, you must accept, don't even have to win it, just have to take it, don't take it and it's seven years of getting gangfucked, so I sez to this fella. no. I reckon you oughtta be stepping aside and he sez yeah? And I sez yeah? And he sez yeah? And I let him have the left hand once, twice, thrice, I give him so many left hands he's begging for the right, and then he goes down hard on the landing, sparko, copious claret all over the place, and I spit on him and I'm about to go on my way, get on the ping pong ,and this old boy, lovely old fella he was, pushing a mop, he says 'Don't leave him like that, son, it'll go on for years and years,' and I reckon he's right, of course. So I straddle the cunt, he's unconscious but his lips are moving like he's making his case, and I pull out this budget bulk-buy sweetcorn lid I bought off the kitchen boys for a coupla phonecards, rusty jagged edge, and I turns his head to one side so I got a clear view of the neck, and he's got this little bird, a swallow in blue and green, good work it was, not rushed, this swallow is right on the vein in the side of the neck, so I sez lovely, that'll guide my hand, and I raise up my other hand with the big lid, 'bout to plunge it up to the hilt when the swallow, and this is no word of it a lie, the swallow turns his face . . . and looks me directly in my eyeball . . . and he sez . . . 'Don't be a cunt all your life, Joseph. Is this how a father's meant to behave? What would Vincent say?' Well, a' course, I'm fuckin' fartfaced, inni? Stumble off him, and stagger off. Guv'nor catches whiff of it, li'l solitary time for me. Well I couldn't have been anywhere better, could I? Ev'ry time they let me out of solo, I bang a screw so's I can go back in there. Took a few beatings off the night shift, but nuffink too calamitous. And you know what I did in that cell on my own? I kept my eyes closed as long as I could and I pictured you. I organised every single memory I had of you. Kept your face in my mind twelve hours a day with my eyes shut for another five years. Didn't want parole, wasn't ready for it ,juss wanted to concentrate on you.

I wanted to send you love somehow . . .

And I know..I know for certain . . . that I reached you from that cell. You must have felt me sometimes. On the breeze . . . Any time you had happy feeling, or felt warm as toast and you couldn't think why . . . That was me, son . . . Loving you in private . . . Always . . .

And I'm glad to be here, even in this unhappy situation, because you know now the love I bear you and you can never take it back . . . I love you beyond the limits of my life . . . Long after I'm gone, you'll be feeling my love . . . My love for you is all I am . . . You're too beautiful for me to do anything but love you. You hear what your old man is telling you? How I meet my maker, bullet or a drop, iss an indifferent,son . . . This love will carry on for ever . . . Beautiful boy. My Beautiful Vincent.

Vincent breaks down.

Vincent They think it was me and it wasn't . . .

Joseph I know . . .

Vincent They're gonna kill me till I'm dead.

Joseph I won't let them.

Vincent I'm so scared . . .

Joseph I know.

Vincent I'm so scared of all the blades.

Joseph You think I'd let some people do anything to you? Y'mad.

Vincent They're so angry at me.

Joseph Let them come.

Vincent They're fixated on me, Mishak sez they've cancelled all other appointments, they're not even gettin' their rent today, juss massive redeployment onto me.

Joseph Don't worry, son. I'll take care of it. Nobody's gonna touch you or your sister.

Vincent Mishak sez he don't wanna know me no more.

Joseph Mishak's weak and I am strong.

Vincent They won't forgive me this time . . .

Joseph Come on, kiddo, get a grip and tell me whass gone wrong. Tell your old man, son.

Vincent Someone's been fiddling with the girl, Rosie.

Joseph Rosie the backwards girl?

Vincent She got pregnant but don't know where babies come from so she never tells nobody till it's too late to fix things. First thing her brothers know she lets out a howl in the laundrette, waters break. Rush her up to UCH, she sets up in the stirrups for two fuckin' days with this baby just wedged inside her, don't wanna come out. Sensible kid, I reckon, musta known what kinda family they are.
  But the doctor's getting worried cause she's weaker and weaker. Then Arnold, he juss decides he'd had enough, soaks his arm in olive oil and puts it right up inside Rosie. The rest a' the family sayin' don't touch your sister like that, but he juss growls at 'em. Pulls the baby out hisself. Doctors, nurses . . . all looking at him. He's got the li'l baby in his arms and he turns to the room and sez he's gonna find the father and he's gonna kill him. Alla the brothers are there, say yeah, fuck yeah,

less kill the man. And thass when Rosie sez my name. Out the fuckin' blue. Completely unwarranted. She juss sez my name. She's got a funny brain, she don't think normal like you and I think normal. She could be saying my name 'cause I gave her a liquorice allsort in nineteen eighty-four or summink. Iss not conclusive proof at all, Joseph. But Arnold and the rest of the Calderazzos take it as Gospel. I wouldn't do that . . . never . . . I done some things that I am so ashamed of, but I would never do that . . . Thass low. Defenceless backwards girl . . . Thass rank . . . I wouldn't do it, Dad. You know that. Don't you?

Joseph Course I do, son. Iss not in your nature.

Vincent Dad, I'm sorry I been so distant from you . . .

Joseph Iss me thass sorry, kid.

Vincent S'all my pride, and all my rage . . .

Joseph Me too. Stupid, 'cause it wastes all that precious time . . .

Vincent And the energy it takes . . .

Joseph Knackering, innit?

Vincent Yeah.

Joseph But there's no going back now, son. I'm in your life again.

Vincent Yeah.

Joseph I'm the person I always threatened to become. I ain't pretending no more. I have roots now. And I'll never turn my back on you again. First things first: where are these Calderazzos living?

Vincent Laundrette's the best bet.

Joseph Laundrette's where the mum is. Am I right?

Vincent Yeah.

Joseph The mum is the key. I'm going straight to her. Whass her name?

Vincent Mrs Calderazzo.

Joseph And the husband? The patriarch?

Vincent The patriarch is not around, I don't reckon.

Joseph Perfect. A widow.

Vincent You gonna sweet her up?

Joseph I'm gonna talk to her parent to parent. She'll hear me. 'Cause this li'l Rosie can't juss call your name and thass it, thass done, you're responsible. They gotta come with DNA, blood samples, all that.

Vincent Thass what I was tryin'a tell 'em, but they wouldn't hear it.

Joseph I'll make her hear it.

Vincent Don't do nuffin bad to them, they're dangerous.

Joseph Don't worry, crazy boy. I'll walk in there with nothing. I'll convince her that I'm real, juss like I done with you. Then I'll 'splain to her how my flesh and blood could never do summink so hostile as to impregnate a li'l slow-learning girl. Tell her the truth: if he's done it, then I'll lay myself across those tracks and wait for the 8.45 for Brondesbury Park to run me over. She'll believe me. No parent could hear what I gotta say and not get behind me.

A long pause.

Tried to see your mum yesterday.

Vincent Wouldn't have it?

Joseph Wouldn't have any of it. Juss cried and cried and cried. She looks squeezed out.

Vincent She'll come round.

Joseph She speaking to you?

Vincent Not for a while. Same thing, looks at me and she's overcome with tears, then she waves me away.

Joseph You can laugh at me if you wanna, but I wanna grow old with that woman. Even after everything.

Vincent I ain't laughing, Dad. I'll help you.

Joseph Lemme see that eyeball of yours, son.

Vincent S'nothing.

Joseph Lemme see it. Looks very distressed.

Vincent It does sting a little bit, Dad.

Joseph Letcha old man take a look.

Vincent goes to him.

Ay, ay, ay, ay, ay . . .

Vincent Looks a lot worse than it is.

Joseph Looks fuckin' bad, mate.

Vincent Kiss it.

Joseph take his head in his hands and kisses his bad eye.

Joseph Funny boy. Crazy boy.

Vincent Things is a little blurred out that peeper.

Joseph It'll go. Arnold's fabled left hook still got the power, I would say, without a doubt.

Pause.

46

Vincent Arnold's fabled left hook?

Pause.

How do you know about Arnold's fabled left hook?

Joseph Isn't that what you said?

Vincent Thass what I said. (*Beat.*) But not to you. I said it to my sister. Nobody else knows I got nailed with the hook. But somehow you know about it.

Joseph What?

Vincent Arnold's fabled left hook.

Joseph Don't spoil it, son . . .

Vincent You said it still got the power, summink like that.

Joseph So?

Vincent Still got the power, like you knew about it before. Like it had power in the past. (*Beat.*) Your statement implied prior knowledge of the power of Arnold's fabled left hook.

Joseph Musta heard someone else talking about it. Mosta Somers know about how devastating that punch is.

Vincent Nah, nah, nah, but . . . You been feeding me soup about how you never heard a' the Calderazzos and who are they and what are they and whass the mum called and now you suddenly tell me about Arnold's fabled left hook.

Pause.

Pieces don't fit, Dad. It doesn't coalesce. Which is it?

Joseph I dunno what you're driving at, son.

47

Vincent Nah, I think you do, Daddy. I think you know full well what I'm driving at. Whass going on? Really and truly. Whass going on?

Whatcha looking at the floor for? Look me in the eye like as if you was a man.

Pause.

Joseph Reckon you caught me out in a li'l fabrication, son.

Vincent Reckon I must have.

Pause.

Joseph I didn't tell you, son . . . It was a Calderazzo that I spared. In prison that time.

Vincent What, the cunt with the tweety-bird on his neck?

Joseph Arnold's baby brother, John. If I'd known, I'd a' killed him, bird or no bird. Bad blood with his lot. Since they flung me in the canal all those years ago.

Joseph lights a smoke.

So I'm coming out now, gates shut behind me, Arnold's there sitting in a Bentley. I'm thinking ambush, but no. He gimme a ride home, says he 'preciates me sparing his baby brother, sez bygones be bygones eh, offers me a position. I respectfully declined him. Got meself a job in a kitchen washing up for some prima donna prick chef thought he was God's gift. But it was good. Felt clean. Til the chef became impolite and I had to tune him up. Stomp outa there thinking whass next, and there he is again. Arnold. Leaning against his Bentley. Waiting for me.

Vincent So you been working for them?

Joseph I'm good at it, son. Thass my tragedy. I juss got this ability to put the damage on a fella. 'S a button.

Press it, do summink horrendous, press it again, go back to the family. Not everyone can do it. And those of us who can do it, we know each other instantly.

Vincent The brotherhood of cunts.

Joseph Then this whole thing comes up with you. Obviously I'm not happy about it. Kicked up a stink with all that lot. Thass when Arnold showed what he's really about. 'We don't know where Vincent is, but we do know where the mum lives.' He said it so cold. I sez, 'What about where the mum lives? Whass your inference?' Arnold juss looked me in the eye, left me in no doubt. So I'm conflicted halfway down my heart. Your mum's led a completely blameless life start to finish. And thass how it ends for her? A visit from the Calderazzos? I walk up the High Street and what do I see? Your mum in Boots arguing about some prescription and geting escorted outa there by the security like some sorta madwoman and I thought . . . iss Vincent's done this, she weren't on no pills before he was born, iss that boy, he's destroyed that woman. You slug. How could I even debate between the loveliness of your mum and you? You might as well be some sorta vermin for all I fuckin' care, son.

Vincent I shoulda put one right behind your earhole when I had the chance.

Joseph You think I wouldna? Thass the difference between you and me. Between man and rat. You got skim-milk for blood. I reckon you ain't even mine. Weak. Whatcha ever given to the world, Vincent? Compared to me?
  I built this block. Cut my hands to ribbons working on this block so's people could live here. This block is me.

Vincent DONCHA KEEP LYING! Sell me to the Calderazzos, I 'spect nuffing else from you, but don't tell me you built this block. Can't stand that. You had fuck-all to do with this block. Arsked Mum about it and she nearly fell off the couch laughing. She tole me the truth, you signed up to work there in the mornin' and by lunchtime you was back in her house, completely fucked. She said you couldn't lift your arms above your head to getcha T-shirt off. You were so fucked you never even picked up your wages. You're a liar, Dad. And you're lazy, and they're pretty much the same thing. And thass the worst thing to call anybody. Lazy.

Joseph Lovely, son. Say everything now, because your life is ebbing away.

Joseph goes to the door.
Vincent blocks his path.

Vincent Where you going?

Joseph Laundrette, get some rat poison.

Vincent You're going to them? You're gonna tell 'em I'm here?

Joseph 'Scuse me.

Vincent blocks his path.

Vincent No.

Pause.

Joseph Heh heh heh . . . What is this, the son must slay the father? How you gonna do that, then? Tell you what, I'll give you a free go at me. Just make sure you don't miss, son.

Pause.
Vincent throws a punch.
Joseph blocks it and headbutts Vincent. Extremely fast.
Vincent drops to the floor.
Joseph locks his arm and twists it.

Ahh . . . Little Vincent had a bang? Let Daddy see it.
That was a nasty knock, wasn't it, kiddo? Come here, son,
lemme tell you a little nursery rhyme . . . This little piggy
went to market . . . (*He breaks Vincent's little finger.*)
This little piggy stayed home . . . (*Breaks next finger.*)
This little piggy had bacon . . . (*Breaks next finger.*)
This little piggy had none . . . (*Breaks finger.*) And this
little piggy . . . This little piggy ran aaaaalllll the way
home. (*Breaks thumb.*) Whassamatter, son, you love that
rhyme . . . Show Daddy where it hurts, Daddy kiss it
better? Hhhmm? Lemme see.

> *Joseph twists his arm.*
> *Vincent writhes in agony.*

I tried everything I could to persuade your mother to
terminate you. Begged her and begged her to abort.
I didn't want no kid, told her you'd be a useless waste
a' life. Bet she fuckin' wishes she'd listened to me now,
steada the priests. She'd kill you like that – (*Snaps
fingers.*) You're nothing to me, son. You're a turd
I dumped in your mother's stomach. Couldn't flush
you till now. You cunt. You nothing. (*Beat.*)
    Calderazzos gonna enjoy you, boy. Down by the
canal. Might even watch them if there's nothing on the
box. (*Beat.*)
    If your grandfather could see you now . . .

> *Joseph lets go of Vincent's arm and kicks him
> extremely hard in the testicles.*
> *Stands over him a moment as Vincent whimpers
> and cries.*
> *Spits on him.*
> *Joseph picks his coat off the back of the chair.*
> *Removes handkerchief and wipes the spittle off his
> chin. Puts coat on.*

Keep the change, Vincent.

Joseph exits.

Vincent slowly pulls himself together, in a lot of pain.

He scrabbles around, wrapping an old shirt of Deirdra's round his hand and tying it tight.

He blows on his fingers to relieve the pain.

Picks up rum bottle, swigs long and hard from it.

Pours rum on his hand to ease the pain.

Opens window.

Blast of cold air, traffic noises, sparks from railway tracks.

Drops empty bottle out of window.

A long pause.

Distant sound of bottle smashing.

Vincent Missed him.

Turns off light.

Three pigeons flutter past the window, startling Vincent and making him jump.

He cranes his head out of the window to see the birds.

Comes back in and closes window.

Enter Deirdra.

Deirdra You OK?

Vincent 'Course I'm OK.

Deirdra You look a little done-in.

Vincent I'm not feeling too clever at the moment, no, Sis.

Deirdra Whass happened to your hand?

Vincent I'm fine.

Deirdra Good.

Vincent Got my bullets, sistren?

Deirdra Yep.

Vincent Give us 'em, then.

> *Deirdra reaches into her coat, takes out a box of bullets.*
> *She begins to hurl them one at a time at Vincent, who ducks for cover.*

Deirdra Here's your fuckin' bullets! How could you do that to that girl! She's learning-disabled! How could you use her like that!

Vincent Ow! Stop flinging them fuckin' bullets at me and less talk it over!

> *Finally she relents.*

Jesus . . . Summink wrong wi' you, y'know that?

Deirdra You're the one got summink wrong with him.

Vincent Whass happened?

Deirdra Coming back from Mishak's, Calderazzos picked me up round Cooper's Lane. The younger ones in the tracksuits. Pulled up in an open-top jeep. Me tryin'a front, act cool, but I'm shitting me knickers. They took me to Mrs Calderazzo, she's sittin' in an old chair. Arnold's there, he's beating the war drum a bit when he sees me, but Mrs Calderazzo juss raises her hands like she's gonna backhand him and there's silence. I'm more scared a' her than any of 'em, but she smiled at me and arxed after my old dear, properly respectful she was, like an old-timer's s'posed to be, said she was sorry to hear she was poorly.

Far off in the back . . . he's crying . . . the nipper . . . But he's not crying juss for so . . . It's deeper. He's crying for the world . . . I never heard no baby sound like that . . . it came from the . . . from the past or summink . . . Mrs Calderazzo sez he cries round the clock, they have

53

to take shifts, nothing will stop him . . . Rosie comes out
through the curtain, sees me, stops and smiles. She got
a beautiful smile, I don't care what nobody says. Comes
over with a doll's brush and combs my hair. I stop myself
from crying but the baby doesn't. Mrs Calderazzo asks
me who the baby sounds like. Looks me right to my
soul. And Rosie says, very simple . . . Vincent. I was
gonna tell her bollocks, my Vincent isn't capable, but the
words juss died in my throat. Couldn't form them. I buss
out crying. Snot flowing, uglyface crying. No denying it.
I didn't have to see Archie to know. Thass your kid out
there.

   Pause.

Vincent What kinda fuckin' proof is that?

Deirdra Women juss know.

Vincent What, 'cause you all bleed once a month, that
makes you psychic?

Deirdra Thass your kid.

   Pause.

Vincent Is he normal? The boy?
   I mean, like . . . he's not a mong or nuffing?

Deirdra He's a healthy baby. And that family love him
up too bad. But that love don't extend to you, Vincent.
Iss juss the reverse, in fact. They can't get over how you
could do that to their sister. And I gotta say, it's a whole
new level you found. Thass spiritual wickedness of the
worst water, Vincent. Thass a real fall from grace.

   Vincent sits down, deflated. He plays with a bullet.

Whatcha gotta say 'bout it, Vincent? Eh?

Vincent Me and Dad had a barny and he's broken my
fingers.

Deirdra Whatcha gotta say about it?

Vincent Forgive me.

Deirdra I don't reckon I will forgive you, Vincent, not this time around, nah.

Vincent What did Mishak say?

Deirdra You think I lissened to that snake?

Vincent He talk to you properly?

Deirdra What I juss tell ya? Clean outcha fucking earhole, Vincent, and stop telling y'self these fuckin' lies. You gimme joke, Vincent. You have reached the bottom of the pit. And you think you're up in the clouds. Cunt.

Vincent Mishak was there as well that night, y'know.

Deirdra How couldjuh have done summink like that? What went through your mind?

Vincent I love you.

Deirdra No, you don't. And if you do, stop it straight away. Don't wanna be loved by you if this is who you are.

Vincent I think I'm not well.

Deirdra I think you're not well. Never heard anything so sick in all my life. Even Mishak wouldn't do nothing like that.

Vincent I love you.

Deirdra What did you do, Vincent?

Vincent I love you.

Deirdra TELL ME WHAT YOU FUCKING DID!

Vincent Coming home late, Mishak's driving, we swing through the square and she's there, Rosie's there in the park burrowing around and eating fuckin' dirt. I don't think Rosie's just a backwards, y'know, thass not the whole thing, I reckon, I think like she's got like . . . nuttiness, or dementedness as well as being a mong, 'cause she's talking stern like she's telling a kid off, and shoutin', like, then laughing and whispering, 's all a bit dark and nasty, like. Angry angry girl.

Deirdra Angry angry girl, tell me what you fucking did.

Vincent Mishak pulls the car over and shines the lights on her through the park and she freezes stock-still, can't even move 'cept for her fingers twitching, I mean, fuck's sakes, Deirdra, that Calderazzo mob they ain't the family they claim to be, what they letting this girl out on her own for? They should be looking after her, Deirdra, not throwing her to the wolves like that.

Deirdra Tell me what you fucking did.

Vincent Sis . . . I juss . . . I . . . I lost all sense a' proportion, thass all . . . Case of bad judgement, Sis . . . Mishak didn't even get out of the car, juss turned the beams on and off full blast, little light show he sez, and he's laughing and telling me go on, boy, give it to her, and I juss . . . I juss gave in, sister. I juss gave in.

Deirdra Gave in? Gave in? Vincent, you give in to a Cadbury's Crunch at lunchtime, you don't give in to summink like that. You don't even think about summink like that. Ain't s'posed to enter your mind.

Vincent I got demons . . .

Deirdra You got demons . . . Ev'ry cunt out there's got demons. No excuse. You do summink, you don't do summink. Thass all there is.
  You and I are no longer brother and sister.
  I hereby unbrother you.

Vincent You can't.

Deirdra Iss done.

Vincent You and me got the same mother.

Deirdra Our same mother is on her fuckin' knees praying for forgiveness 'cause she don't know what she done wrong. To have a first-born carry on like that. The suffering you've caused her . . . Not being funny, right, but you're a little fucked-up in the head, Vincent, I'm sorry, but thass the God's honest truth and you know it is. Summink wrong with you, summink holding you back, not like Rosie, but summink holding you back from being normal and you know iss true. (*Beat.*) I told 'em you're up here, Vincent.

Pause.

Vincent Thass cold, D.

Deirdra I don't feel no way 'bout if iss cold. If iss cold, iss cold. Ain't for you to warm me up. Biological don't matter. Iss a lie that you can't pick your family, you can. And you can unpick it. And thass what I'm choosing to do.

Vincent You used to idolise me. When they said to you, whadjuh wanna be, pumpkin? You used to say I wanna be Vincent.

Deirdra The Calderazzos will be here soon, the lotta them. Think they said summink about driving you down to the canal.

Vincent It was me that gave you that name. Pumpkin. I coined it. Not your dad. He went with it 'cause he loved to call you that.

Deirdra You want my advice, juss take the pain with the minimum of fuss. That way you might live on. I'm done. Thass it. The whole thing's done. Your childhood is over.

Vincent picks up his gun and opens the chamber.

Whatcha doing?

Vincent Blaze a' glory time, D. Watch me make it rain.

Deirdra Oh, don't give me that . . .

Vincent Fuck it. I don't wanna be some brain-damaged cripple limping round Somers for them to point at and tell tales about. Fuck it. Pass me the ammo.

Deirdra Vincent, you'll shoot up my flat . . .

Vincent Do you a big favour. Council getcha a transfer off the Tower. Move you up in the world to Queen's Crescent. Should be thanking me, D. Pass me the bullets.

　Pause.

Deirdra Hope you choke on these fuckin' bullets, Vincent. (*Deirdra passes him the bullets.*)

Vincent Nice big box. With a bit a' luck I'll take a lot of them with me, long as I can reload quick. Shame I can't get this kid they keep clucking over. Thass not the legacy I wanna have living on after I'm gone, half-idiot spastic boy being raised by that mob, no thank you very much. Wanted to present Mum with a proper grandson one day, but fuck it . . .

　Vincent clicks open his gun. Everything is extremely awkward with his broken hand.

I reckon I could get 'em as they come out the lift, they won't be ready for that, they don't even know I'm armed, then I can pull back into here, shut the door, reload, pick a few off. They might get hold a' me in the long term, but gristle will fly, boy, gristle will fucking fly. I will change their family portrait for ever, telling you . . . (*He tries to load the gun. The bullets don't fit.*) That fuckin' Mishak McCormack . . .

Deirdra Whassamatter?

Vincent Bullets don't fit.

Deirdra What?

Vincent They don't fit. Fuckin' wrong size.

Deirdra You're joking.

Vincent Sold us the wrong bullets. How much he charge you?

Deirdra He's your friend, not mine . . .

Vincent AIN'T EVEN GOT A FUCKIN' FRIEND! NO SISTER, NO FATHER, NO FUCKER IN THE WORLD WANTS TO HELP ME! YOU PUT THAT FUCKIN' APE CALDERAZZO FAMILY AHEAD OF YOUR OWN! AINTCHA HEARD OF FUCKIN LOYALTY?

> *Beat.*

Nothing. Nothing. Nothing.
　　Why is it always me that gets the blame? Am I cursed? Is this a curse? I done summink heinous in a previous life? Why am I not forgiven?

> *Beat.*

Fuckin' Mishak McCormack.

Deirdra This ain't about Mishak.

Vincent Yes, it is, he's a bad influence on me. Everyone at school told me not to move with him and I knew it as well. But he come to me, y'know. Juss said he really liked me and we should be mates. Juss like that. Now look. No fuckin' sense a' personal responsibility whatsoever. Never had one and he never will.

Deirdra This ain't about Mishak.

Vincent I'm never speaking to him again as long as I live.

Deirdra Mishak's not the problem.

Vincent Is it cold in here, or is it juss me?

Deirdra It's juss you, Vincent. (*Beat.*) One thing I'm positive about . . . It's definitely juss you.

Knock on the door.

Vincent Get in the bathroom.

Deirdra gets in the bathroom.
 Vincent picks up a kitchen knife.
 Door swings open.
 Joseph enters, bloody clothes, carrying an infant baby, heavily wrapped up.

Joseph Anybody in?

Vincent Thought I toldjuh to leave me alone.

Joseph Look what I done for you. (*He proffers the baby.*)

Vincent Whassat?

Joseph This is Archie.

Vincent Whass Archie gotta do wimme?

Joseph Don't be silly, kiddo. Archie got ev'rything to do with you. Look at him. Look at the little guv'nor. Eh? Ain't he a beauty?

Vincent Whatcha done, Dad? You gone wading in? Why is there blood?

Joseph Thass my blood. Not Archie's.

Vincent What the fuck you done bringing this li'l snail round to me? I don't want it.

Joseph I dunno, son, I'm still tryin'a sort it out in my own head. When I left here. I know you flung that bottle at me, you lairy so-and-so, I spin round see three pigeons you'd upset flapping up past your window, passed Deirdra on the way out, she never noticed, bit preoccupied,

I reckon. In the laundrette now, the mum lets me in, goes to get Arnold, and I'm in the room with the li'l fella, he's cryin' and cryin' and cryin' and I'm on my own so I pick him up . . . Vincent . . . I did the earhole thing I showed to you . . . and the li'l fella . . . calmed down straight away . . . just the way you did, my darling boy . . . Big moment for a man like me, lemme tell yuh . . .

I realised in a flash that I couldn't fuck up my li'l boy's life like I planned to, there's rules about that sorta thing, son . . . Asked Arnold if there wasn't an alternative. I even offered up your hand in marriage, desperate measure, son, you know how it goes, said you'd marry Rosie and live in the laundrette with the mum.

Arnold waved the proposal away, He has to die, mate, I'm sorry. Didn't even consider it for a moment. And thass when I hit the button. Tried talking, didn't work, so go for what you know. Heart's only slowing down now. But I got the boy. I got him out of what I reckon would have been a very repressive environment.

Vincent What did you do over there?

Joseph I'm not even sure. I hit the button and I laid waste to some cunts.

Vincent You laid waste to the Calderazzos?

Joseph At least five of 'em, son, yeah.

Vincent Fuck's sakes . . .

Joseph It was a red mist, son, what can I say?

Vincent What the fuck I'm s'posed to do with this? This is juss a shit factory.

Joseph Look . . . even managed to bring up his formula. (*Joseph pulls out some baby formula.*) Poor cow, the Rosie girl ain't got the good milk. Archie don't wanna know about the paps. Poor girl can't bring up a child. Iss not right, son.

Vincent I don't want this.

Joseph Yes, you do. Juss in shock, son, thass all. Can't take it in and thass completely human of you.

Vincent Take the kid back. This juss makes it worse.

Joseph Nah, son. This makes it one hundred per cent better. Said I would, didn't I? All you have to do . . . is look the kid in the eyeball. And you'll know. Juss like I knew.

> *He hands the baby over to Vincent.*
> *Vincent looks at the baby.*

Vincent I don't think this kid's too well. He looks disgruntled.

Joseph He's juss working out who you are, son.
 Seen this telly show once when I was downstairs, not this time, the time previous, these psychiatrists reckoned at this age they think that all other humans are figments of their imagination. They think that they've created their mum and dad, steada the other way round. Int'resting, innit? Of course, in some sense this is true. He's made you into summink that you weren't before he was born, so he has created you, he's created a new person as well as being a new person hisself. They're the ones in charge. This little beautiful little pumpkin butternut creature is the master of all he surveys. Had murders tryin'a keep that show on, all the others wanted to check out *Crimewatch* or somesuch. Some people juss don't wanna evolve, do they? (*Beat.*) You got a fag, son?

Vincent Ain't s'posed to smoke round the baby. Bad for his lungs.

Joseph Less open the window, then.

Vincent You mad? Fuckin' cold breeze up here'll kill the little fella.

Joseph Oh. Right you are, then.

Vincent Look at the little fella.

Joseph Quite a little parcel, in' he?

Vincent He's beautiful . . .

Joseph You'll do alright. I can tell. Feel his head. Feel the ridge. See? Thass the same ridge. Touch my head, son. Go on, touch it . . . See?

Vincent Fuckin' hell . . .

Joseph Fuckin' brings you up short, dunnit, son?

Vincent Fucking hell . . .

Joseph Whass happened to your hand, son?

Vincent Caught in a door, Dad.

Joseph Looks nasty.

Vincent Deirdra, come out here.

Joseph Deirdra's here?

Vincent In the bathroom. Got the hump a li'l bit.

Joseph Come out here, darling. See what I broughtcha.

Pause.
Deirdra emerges. She sees the baby.

Deirdra Oh my God . . .

Vincent Eh? You ever seen the like, Sis?

Deirdra Oh my God . . .

Vincent Eh? Eh?

Deirdra He juss, he juss . . . overwhelms you, don't he? He's a little fucking . . . Look at him, oh my God . . .

Vincent Eh? Little terrorist. My son. Hahahaha.

63

Deirdra Look at his li'l hands and feet . . .

Joseph Look at the ears.

Deirdra Oh my God, I'm gonna fuckin' cry. Fuckin' hell. Look at the little fucker.

Vincent This kid's gonna have a future. Got talent dripping off him.

Deirdra Lemme hold him.

Vincent No.

Deirdra Come on, gi's a go.

Joseph Not yet, love. Let him hold him.

Vincent Where's that bottle?

Joseph Here y'are, son.

Vincent Ta.

Deirdra Look at him suck that down.

Joseph Hehehheh . . .

Vincent Where does he put it?

Joseph Gonna be a thoroughbred. Intya? Li'l thoroughbred.

Deirdra I reckon he sorta favours our mum, Vee.

Vincent Lemme see.

Joseph Fuck me.

Deirdra See what I mean?

Vincent He does! Thass weird! He does!

Joseph Thass fuckin' uncanny . . .

Vincent My li'l seedling? Intya? My li'l acorn.

Deirdra Who's got a fag? I'm roasting.

Joseph Vincent sez not around the li'l un.

Deirdra Oh course. Sorry, Dad.

Joseph Thass alright, girl.

Vincent My boy. The violinist. The nine-point-six-second hundred-metre man. The star. The apex. Come to run this manor, come to run all the man dem from Camden. The world stopped spinning when you was born, son. You juss gotta give us the word, and it'll rotate again.

Deirdra He's perfection. I'm gonna fuckin' cry, I swear to God, I've wet my fuckin' knickers, this child's so perfect.

Joseph Full back for Tottenham Hotspur.

A knocking on the door.

Vincent Listen to me, boy. Listen very carefully to what I'm about to say. There's nobody better than you. Not on this earth, not one man or woman. Nobody. No king, no queen. Nothing comes before you. Juss so you know. Juss so you heard, because this is what you need to hear. You can do anything you want to with your time on this planet, truss. I'll be there to help you do it. I'm not going anywhere. I'm not taking one step from your side. Ever.

The knocking continues.

Joseph I can't tell you what it does to a man when he's presented with a grandson. It's a unique pride. And in this block that I built. My grandson is nourished in the block I busted my bollocks to erect. I live on through this boy. Just as I live on through this block.

The knocking continues.

Vincent A fitting monument, Dad.

Joseph Thank you, son.

Deirdra He's smiling at me. Aren't you? Yes, you are. Little bubba. You smilin at you aunty-waunty, so you are.

Vincent Anything you feel, I'm gonna know it. And I'll guide you through anything. I will always know what to tell you whenever you feel a feeling that scares you.

The knocking builds.

And I know you'll speak well of me when I'm gone, son, I'll make sure a' that. When people ask you about your old man, you're gonna choke with tears and swell with pride. You're gonna tell 'em, 'My dad was a mighty oak tree. I could see him for miles. No matter where I went. Look back and see my dad. Solid.' And you know what, son? You'll be right.

Joseph hangs his head. He puts a solemn hand on Vincent's shoulder.
More knocking.

Joseph This is what I wanted all along. For us to be together like this. The whole family. What a shame your mum's not ready for us.

Deirdra She will. When she gets a loada this little fella, she'll melt.

Joseph opens up his jacket. He has four guns in holsters.

Joseph Here y'are, son, get hold a' one a' these. This one, the Nine . . . That goes with that box a' bullets you got on the table. Mishak soldja them? For that old Webley? He's a born piss-taker, that lad. Have two, go on.

Vincent You had those on you all the time?

Joseph Thass like asking if I take air in my lungs when I breathe, son.

Vincent You sly old fox. You sat here with all that under your coat and you never let on?

Joseph Come here, boy, give your old dad a cuddle.

Vincent falls onto the sofa and cuddles his dad.

You too, girl.

Deirdra What?

Joseph Come and get some a' this love, eh, girl.

She falls onto the sofa and joins in the hug.

Eh? Eh? Who can you turn to? Eh? I toldjuh I'd put things right. Always listen to Daddy . . .

The knocking builds and builds and builds until it intensifies into loud and hefty kickings.

    The family are seemingly oblivious, Vincent slowly loading his gun, Joseph and Deirdra looking lovingly at the baby, Joseph making silly faces at it and giggling.

    The door shudders, but holds.

    Blackout.

    End.